“Neil Schambra St … about
work/life balance t … ny and
does so in a way th … an.”

Claus Raasted
Director, The College of Extraordinary Experiences

“A Bad Hand Played Well’ is a timely guide, offering accessible insights to enable a strong resilient mindset for yourself, to thrive in these challenging times. To find harmony with life and work and to live with kindness and intention every day.”

Ozlem Tuskan
Founder & Chief Executive Officer, The Resilient

“Inspiring, insightful and full of realistic and actionable optimism. A book for better navigating these new normal complex times, starting first with ourselves and then connecting with other people to share the journey to make change happen together.”

Alessio Cuccu
Chief Kindness Officer, Kindnovate

A Bad Hand Played Well' has a really nice perspective, away from victim play or anger. A solutions focused book where you feel a bit more in control of your life and how to change it."

Gabrielle van Asselt
Associate Design Partner, Unknown

'A Bad Hand Played Well' reminds me of the simple truth. Just do the things you can't resist doing. Then do more of it. And do it often. This will take me to the places where I make a difference unique to me."

Gordon Euchler
Founder, The 30 Minute University of Planning

"Neil is a true visionary for those seeking a fresh perspective on their working life and this book is a game changer. A thought provoking must-read for anyone curious about how to reconfigure their working world."

Shamila Mhearban
Executive Coach, Forbes Coaches Council

‘A Bad Hand Played Well’ offers new insights for individuals and teams to create dynamic, kinder ways for people to thrive at work. In the words of the late, great Joe Strummer “Without people, you’re nothing.””

Raoul Shah
Founder, Exposure

“Neil celebrates kindness by emphasizing its importance in everyday life. In particular why we can, should and must bring this important act into the workplace, in order to move the needle on organizational culture and business results. In his words ‘the future of business is kind.’”

Monika Michaliszyn
Vice President, Human Resources (People Services), VF EMEA

“Neil is a coach who will empower you to use the hand you’ve been dealt, not just in your work but in every facet of life.

Minesh Siyani
Learning + Development Lead, Wieden + Kennedy

"A great book by a former C Suite executive who shares tangible examples on how you can start today by starting small. These insights can be life changing and bring joy in how you go about spending those 90,000 hours at work".

Kobi Ampoma
Head of Talent Acquisition, The Heineken Company

"Neil highlights so many of the qualities that help a manager become a leader of people. These are not soft, esoteric ideas, but rather real and practical insights that can make us better at work, and happier as people."

Jeff Shafer
Chief Communications Officer and Vice President of Corporate Marketing Group, Lenovo

“Neil’s book is transformative. He doesn’t just break the rules; he gives us kinder, more human ones to follow instead.
“A Bad Hand Played Well” serves as our call to adventure, our new manifesto for kindness not only to ourselves, but to each other. “The future of business is kind.” And I, for one, welcome that future.”

Brian Págan
Founder, The Greatness Studio

“90,000 hours sounds like a lot. It sounds like enough to master nine different paths. Enough to try everything you’ve ever wanted to try. What a joy to imagine 90,000 hours of freedom. But what a terror to imagine your 90,000 hours owned by someone else.
And the difference between the two?
Taking ownership of how you play your hand.”

Helen King
Creative Director, adidas

A Bad Hand Played Well

How To Own Your 90,000 Hours At Work

Neil Schambra Stevens

MERCURY
JAM

A Bad Hand Played Well

Printed by: KDP Print

ISBN: 978-90-833676-0-6

Mercury Jam Coaching

https://www.mercuryjam.com

Contents

Dedications

Mum was a poet:
she lived a life full of words.
Every day Mum saw joy, and she saw joy in the everyday.
Sadly, when it was her time the universe spoke;
she passed away on World Poetry Day 2022.
This book is dedicated to her, with love.
Words mattered to her, and they matter to me too.

"Nothing that is loved, fades into forgetfulness."

To Zack and Ray,
Proud and excited to see how you choose
to spend your 90,000 hours.
Love, Dad.

Introduction

Let's start at the end.

Every human is connected by one thing.
At some point we will take our last breath
and pass away.

That might not seem the most uplifting start of a book.
It is intentionally there to trigger a jolt, to get a reaction.

Hopefully it will inspire some positive thoughts and importantly, action about how we choose to live our lives.

Or to put it another way:
if you don't do it when you're alive,
when are you going to do it?

On average we spend 90,000 hours of our lives working.
The only thing we spend more time doing is sleep.

How we spend our time at work,
the value we get from it,
the meaning we attach to it,
is something that has been debated for years.

Accelerated by the pandemic,
the system is broken.
The traditional way of working,
gone forever.

The days of the one-company career, the stability of generations before us, long gone.

We can no longer rely
on companies to guarantee our futures.
Or our happiness.

It is now on us as individuals to make a change.
'*Life is a bad hand played well*' might sound harsh.
But for many, their work environments are damaging.

The impact of toxicity is widespread.
On people and companies alike.

75% of Gen-Z's have left a company due to mental health concerns (choosing to put their well-being ahead of the company.)

One in six of the working population of The Netherlands are currently out on burnout (that's a post pandemic figure.)

57% of U.S. and Canadian workers feel stressed on a daily basis. (The highest in the world.)

The impact of mental health and burnout costs the
UK economy £35 billion annually
(meaning mental health problems cost £1,300 for
every employee in the UK economy.)

And the impact on the global economy is over a $1 trillion each year (every single year.)

Knowing all this,
why would we continue working in the same way?
We have one life to live.
Let's make it a good one -
on our terms.

The aim of this book is to give you hope and permission
to look at things differently.

To rethink how you use those precious hours.
To take back control of your working journey
and bring joy to your daily life.

There is choice.
There is freedom.
There is opportunity.

We can pick and choose.
We can work in an office.
We can work remotely.
There are multiple options.
The choice of how we spend those 90,000 hours is up to us.

This book is intended to be a guide.
Yes, it offers facts and figures, with anecdotes and stories
to hopefully spark optimism and ideas.
However, the underlying theme
the main point, is that we have one life.
Let's figure out the best way to enjoy this time.

To invest in you.
To live those hours
with the certainty that we know how this story ends.

As Steve Jobs famously said:
"Being the richest man in the cemetery doesn't matter to me."

Seize the opportunity.
Make a choice.
Figure out what your passion is,
decide what matters to you
and just go for it.

And if you're not sure,
Try something. Start something.
Explore.
There's enough time.
Just don't waste it.

Chapter 1.

It All Starts With You

"Just as time knew to move on since the beginning,
and the seasons know exactly when to change.
Just as kindness knows no shame,
know through all your joy and pain,
that I'll be loving you always."

Stevie Wonder - 'As'

This is a book about work.
Except it isn't really.
It's a book about you.
Your life.

Your relationship with work
and how you spend
your 90,000 working hours.

It's about taking care of yourself,
putting your needs first.
By no means in a selfish way.

If you are not in a good place
physically or mentally,
then it's hard to show up
and be there for others.

It's about looking out for number one,
navigating the highs and the lows,
the joy and the pain,
ensuring that you are loving yourself
always.

Sometimes Things Fall Apart

They say there are four major stress triggers in life:

Losing a job.
Bereavement of a close family member.
Marriage or divorce.
Moving house.

I experienced all four
in under a year
in the midst of a global pandemic.

This experience taught me *resilience*
and to never give up.
Momentum - always keep moving forwards.
The importance of demonstrating
actionable kindness,
and *gratitude.*

These are the *four founding principles*
of my coaching consultancy, Mercury Jam.
By focusing on people,
and enabling them to *be seen, heard and valued.*

I couldn't be happier
or more energised.
It shows that sometimes
everything has to completely fall apart
- to unravel -
to find out where
you're truly meant to be in life.

Choose Kindness

Be someone who is open to see the love and kindness that is everywhere.

For many years, I've been getting up early, to walk and explore the city where I live. Taking twists and turns away from the main drag, I often find myself in sleepy back streets, away from the hustle and bustle, the touristy squares.

Alone with my thoughts, captivated by the light, I start to see things differently. Quite literally. Kindness and love can sneak up on you.
It can be unexpected. However, once you have experienced it, it's hard to turn away.

That is because kindness is not random. It's an intention.
An action. A mindset.

Once you make the choice, you see it, feel it everywhere.
And then you will know it is the right door for you to knock on.

What do you see today?

"Kindness is a language which the deaf can hear and the blind can see"

Christian Nestell Bovee

Celebrate Your Domino Days

I'm a firm believer in everything for a reason.

Often things might not seem obvious
in that moment,
be it particular thoughts, words or incidents.
A shared interaction.
A chance meeting or introduction.

This is the nature of everyday life and life every day.
However, in time things manifest themselves
in seemingly unconnected and unrelated ways.

This connection is an exciting moment.
Be it a conversation,
a new introduction,
an unexpected response,
whatever the physical or verbal manifestation may be.

I call these moments 'Domino Days.'

It is when, like dominoes, one thing triggers another.
There is a ripple, a domino effect if you will,
that builds momentum,
that sets us off on a new path or journey.

It creates new opportunities.
It generates impetus and energy.
A potential catalyst to something new and exciting.

'Domino Days' don't happen that often.
When they do,
they should be acknowledged,
celebrated.

Really celebrated.
They are a reminder
that we are part of something
bigger.

That the universe is truly aligned,
and that it confirms our belief in
everything for a reason.

Choices

Faced with

death,

divorce,

and the geographical distance from my children.

I choose

peace,

love,

and kindness.

Put Life First

June 21.
Summer solstice.
The longest day of the year.

For a while now
I've been tracking the lunar cycles,
and the impact that planetary movements
have on our wellbeing.
It's fascinating.

Nature and the universe are out there.
It is all around us.
We humans are merely guests.

Yet how many of us
put our work first, above all else,
when we should be putting life first,
and how we spend
our time on this beautiful planet.

None of us,
not even the perceived
'most powerful' people on Earth
can alter the turning of the tides,
the sun rising and setting,
or the cycles of the moon.

We are merely witnesses
to this amazing spectacle
that happens regardless,
with or without us.
Yet we put the importance of work on such a high pedestal.

Even on the day that celebrates
the halfway point of yet another year.

Why not take the opportunity to reflect,
To look ahead.
To find balance.

And to prioritise the most important things in your life.

Thought For The Day

If you can't be kind today, scroll on.

Fly At Your Own Frequency

Winston Churchill famously said;
"If you're going through hell, keep going."

There will always be those
who don't appreciate you.
That toxic line manager,
co-worker or employee.

They don't recognise your value,
your purpose,
what you bring to the table.

Sadly, for many
this can trigger anxiety,
a lack of self-worth.
It dents our confidence.

Easier said than done at times,
however, we need to maintain
our true path and passion.

Keeping flying
at your own level,
with your own integrity.

Keep thinking
at a positive frequency.
And just keep going.

If you can maintain
your resilience and your belief,
things will get better.

Indeed.
All will be well.

Just keep flying.

The First Time

You only have to do something
for the first time,
once.

Sometimes the biggest obstacle
to doing something is ourselves.
We are our biggest stumbling block.

There's another five second rule.
Not the one about dropping food on the floor,
or whether toast always lands facedown.

It's the five seconds before our cognitive process kicks in.

1, 2, 3, 4, 5.

In those moments
our brain clicks into gear.
We begin
the cycle of questioning,
of overthinking things.

I'm not encouraging recklessness and irrational actions here.

However just starting something,
putting one foot in front of the other,
reaching out to someone
with a text or call,
is enough to trigger a response,
an emotion or an action.

Which in turn opens doors
and opportunities.
You just don't know
until you try.

Why not give it a whirl?

Choose Life Today

It's always a good day for making memories.
Don't let anyone tell you otherwise.

Joy Seeks World

Mum didn't like fuss...

She didn't appreciate superfluous noise.
She had little patience for what she would describe as 'yawping';
those speaking in loud, ill-considered tones.
She certainly didn't tolerate words
being used unkindly.

You see, words were one of her great joys.

It felt that anything
that got in the way of that
was extra,
a distraction.
The right words were enough.

Mum was a calm, gentle, serene soul.
Very private in many ways.
However, don't be fooled.
Inside there burned a desire
to express her world as she saw it.

Simplicity and complexity
went hand in hand.
She wrestled and agonised
over which
beautifully crafted word to use.
To describe her observations and appreciation
of family, faith, and nature.

Even in her later years
with her mobility compromised,
she would say that inside she was still sixteen,
running across Roughdown Common.
An untamed desire
to be free with her words and nature.

Every day Mum saw joy,
and she saw joy in the everyday.
She reveled in its beauty
with an almost childlike awe.
She would try her utmost

to encourage you
to join in her celebration
of this joy and wonder.

One of Mum's many gifts
was her ability to show you that,
no matter how hard things
seemed at times,
you only needed
to look out of a window
or go for a walk,
to see how much beauty
there was in the natural world.

Mum's poem "*Suitable Gifts*"
highlights her love of nature.

It reminds us that the simplest pleasures in life,
can often bring us
the greatest reward and joy.

"Suitable Gifts"

by Jean Marian Stevens

When I am old,
please do not bring me sweets,
(Soft ones, my dears, in deference to my teeth)
Or pale pink soap,
or flasks of tepid scent.
Not even slippers,
gentle to slow feet.

Bring me berries from some rampant hedge,
Or beech leaves,
shrieking the return of Spring.
Lupins aflame with rain,
or damp,
dark moss,
Cloistered in woods and smelling of the pines.

Keep your slim rosebuds,
lovely as they are,
But bring me clover,
cowslips,
campion.

And,
failing all,
a handful of wet earth,
That I may breathe its wholeness and be free.

Rest Is Productive

"I'd probably say Magnolia."

"Good choice,
and what is it that you love about Magnolia?" I asked.

"The beautiful big floppy petals the color and the shape,
just says spring to me," the client replied.

"And when does the Magnolia bloom?"
"Probably around late March..."

"Sure," I replied,
"but it doesn't last long, does it? A few weeks maximum?
And then often a high wind will come along
and scatter those beautiful petals.
We still get to enjoy them but they're on the floor.
Like big, fluffy potato chips.

And what about for the rest of the year?" I asked.

"Well, they have this lovely
big kind of green waxy leaves that I enjoy looking at."

"So, the thing that the Magnolia is known for,
these beautiful flowers,
it only lasts for a relatively short period of time?" I pressed.

"Yes, I suppose so.
I hadn't thought about it like that."
said the client.

The point here is
that we don't always have to be busy,
to be always on,
to be known for something.

There is equal value
in investing time
in rest and recovery.
Taking inspiration from nature

to be fallow,
to be dormant,
on occasion to just be.

Because just being
is an important part of growth.

As humans our aim
is to grow,
to flourish,
to thrive.
But we can't do that at the same pace,
all the time.

We need to build in moments
to rest.
To recover.
To just be.

In the context of work,
it's the difference between
being busy

and being productive.
Ultimately being productive
delivers greater results.
If you're thinking
that by
not being busy,
not doing something
all the time,
you are not contributing
to your growth and development,
think again.

By using vital time and energy
to churn and burn
through your day,
you're doing yourself a disservice.

Instead,
take a moment.
Just be,
because that is also contributing
to your growth and development.

It just feels different.
That's all.
Be present, now.

It's Okay To Be Messy, Life Is Messy Too

Façade is a powerful word.
There is this façade,
this veneer,
this superficial element
in life and business today.

There's an expectation
that everything must be polished,
presented just so.

To be refined in a particular way
which for a lot of us,
doesn't actually ring true.
We don't live in an Instagram bubble.

People on Instagram,
don't live on Instagram.
Our lives are different.
Our lives are messy,
clumsy, disorganised.

They are not always so refined and clear.
And that's okay.
Clumsy is okay.
Not necessarily always having a clear path is okay.

In those moments,
check yourself.
Remember where you are
on your journey.
Keep your eyes on the prize.
Your prize.

All will be well.

Patience Wins

Sometimes we're looking
in the wrong place,
at the wrong moment.
Or knocking
on the wrong door,
at the wrong time.

What is meant to be will not pass you by.
If it didn't open, it's not your door.
Don't give up.
It's just a matter of time
for things to work out in your favour.

Be patient.
Everything for a reason.
Keep going.

90,000 Hours

Decisions are often made
without our input or involvement,
especially in business.

Things that happen around us
or impact our day to day,
promotions or layoffs for example.

It is up to us
how we respond in that moment.
How much energy we expend.
How much of a sense of control
we feel
is entirely on us.

Not releasing that control
or giving away energy.
Holding onto our emotions.

Retaining
what's important to us,
our values,
we don't have to give that up.

The impact of a decision
might not be something
we asked for
or wished for.

How we deal with it
in that moment,
how we respond,
is entirely on us.

It can be easy to dwell
on a specific point
or moment in time,
to ask ourselves
what we should
have done differently,
or could
have done differently.

It can be a natural reaction.

At this point, pull back.
Refocus on the big picture.
Envision your 90,000 hours.
And how you want to spend them.

Be bold.
Be kind.
Be well.

It's Okay Not To Know

"I don't know."

How often do we say
these words out loud at work?
Not often enough.

The expectation of having all the answers,
all the time at work,
is just unrealistic.
It adds an extra level of pressure
and stress
which we don't need.

Outside of the workplace,
do you always know the answer to every question?
Definitely not.

It's human nature to pause, to question.
To be curious, to ask, to learn.
To be uncertain of something.

It's just who we are,
how we're made up.
Breathe,
step forward,
be yourself.

Persevere

Persevere.

Growth is hard.
Ask a plant.

It might not feel like your surroundings
are always nurturing and supporting you.
However, your head and heart know what to do.
Keep going – you'll get there.

Wet And Wise

There are 101 reasons you can think of not to do it.
But you'll never regret going for a swim.

Just Be You

A post about posting.
AKA the 'Seinfeld' post.

Somedays I feel the pressure
to put content out there.
But my heart and soul
just aren't into it, and the recipient or reader will feel it.

So, listen to yourself.
It's okay not to be always 'on.'

Anyone else have those days?

Your Cup

It can be hard to acknowledge
how we really feel.

All too often we ask,
"How are you?"
The response is usually a mundane
"OK" or *"Good, you?"*
If we're lucky, we get a *"Great!"*

There's a reluctance
to open up,
to share.

Try this instead.
It's a simple visualisation technique
to describe how we're feeling
on any given day.

Rather than asking
"How are you?",
ask
"How is your cup today?"

That may sound strange.
Bear with me.

The 'today' part is important;
it grounds us
in the moment,
in the now.

By visualising
our feelings as a cup,
it allows us to put things into context.

Let's start with the size of the cup.
If we're feeling
positive and energised
the cup might be large.

If we are lacking in something
in that moment,
on that day,
our cup
might be significantly
smaller.

The second criteria:
"How full is your cup?"

The goal here is to
define the fullness
by a specific amount
of water in the cup.

Imagine
there is a finite
amount of water
each day.

The first person
who needs to
drink the water
is ourselves.

We need to ensure
that we have
sufficient
to quench our thirst.

For if we are not kind
to ourselves first,
it is difficult for us
to be useful and supportive
to others.

We then visualise
how much water
we need for ourselves
and how much there is left
to share with others,
be it family,
friends,
co-workers.

By visualising
your feelings
in terms of a size
of a cup,
and how much water
or how full the cup is,
it allows us
to express ourselves
more openly.

It allows for authenticity
and vulnerability,
in a way that we don't necessarily feel overexposed.
For example,
if someone describes
their cup as large,
overflowing with enough water to quench multiple
people
then we know
what kind of mood
we are in that day.

Similarly, if someone
describes
their cup as small,
half full
with only enough
water for themselves
it is an indication
that we might need

to lean in,
to inquire further
as to their well-being.
Alternatively,
to give them a little space and grace.

The fun part is
we get a new cup every day.

We start each day afresh
and this allows us to focus on being present,
on being in the now.

Visually it gives us an opportunity
to assess where we are
on a given day,
or week, month or year.

Our cup might be bigger,
or smaller,
or more,
or less full
from one day to the next.
It's more real,
more authentic,
more personable,
more human approach to connection.

And that is a much better way
of articulating our feelings than
"How are you?"

Gratitude Not Attitude

Never forget,
the world owes you nothing.

Yet it can give you everything.
Open your heart and open your mind.
Remind yourself
to practice gratitude
not attitude.

Why Words Matter

"I'm sitting at the dining room table
looking out onto the front garden."

This was the opening
to pretty much all the letters
I received from Mum.

From the age of about twenty,
for the next 30 years or so,
she wrote to me
at least once a week, if not more.
She did the same for my two older sisters.

Wherever I was in the world,
the UK, the Netherlands,
the US or Italy,
she would send a handwritten letter.

After the opening,
the next few sentences
would probably be about a particular bird
(likely a blackbird, thrush or similar)
who was hopping about in the garden,
followed by a brief description
of the weather that day.

The familiarity of the scene,
the connection to home,
was grounding.
The consistency,
welcoming.

It was only later in life,
with her mobility compromised,
that the letters stopped.

She still wrote
her own Christmas cards and birthday cards.
Always by hand,
always the beautiful,
distinctive writing.

The first birthday
after she passed away,
a thing that hit me hard
was the reality
that I would never
receive a card
or letter from her again.

I would never see
that beautiful handwriting,
or the sign off
'With much love, Mum.'

In a world
where we are consumed
by speed and screens,
sometimes a small reminder
of the human touch
is all it takes.

To remind us
of the fragility of life.

The importance
of living each day
to its fullest.

We only get one life.
Make it a good one.

Give And Glow

Make a choice
to spend time today
with people who give and glow.

Don't concede your energy
to the 'haters and takers.'
You know who they are.

Everything For A Reason

There are times when we pause.

These can be moments
during the day.
At the weekend.
During the holidays.

It could be an extended period
away from work,
whether that is something
we have chosen to do,
or we find ourselves in that situation
due to redundancy or layoffs.

In that moment,
however brief,
it is an opportunity for us to breathe,
to embrace life.

It is an opportunity
to relearn how to live,
versus learning how to work.

We are not defined by our jobs or title.
Working forms part of our lives.
It is not our entirety.

When we are born,
we learn to move,
to walk, to talk,
to feed ourselves.

Our appetite
for learning and discovery
should continue
throughout our lives.
Even to our final breath.

In our latter years
there is still much to learn,
wisdom and reflection to share.

Life is a bad hand played well.
It is much more than the hours
that we commit
to this thing called 'work.'

There is an abundance of wonder out there.
We choose our mindset,
and how receptive we are to it.

Life is about making memories.
Creating experiences.
There is nothing transactional about that.

Be Ready

'Wake me up when I'm famous.'
Stay humble, stay focused.
Persevere.
Be consistent,
play the long game.

Check the backstory
of those individuals or brands,
who are labeled
an 'overnight success.'

The reality is usually something different.

They mentally invested in themselves.
They believed in their goal or mission.
Kept it simple.
Kept plugging away.

Often for years,
before something clicked,
or fell into place.

You don't know
when that moment will be,
just be ready
to '*shine your light*'.

Because You Can

Breakfast for dinner,
is always a winner.

Chapter 2.

Navigating Work

"You can't always get what you want.
But, if you try some time,
you'll find you get what you need."

The Rolling Stones - "You Can't Always Get What You Want"

A lot of my work as a coach
is focused on two areas with clients:
vision and pain points.

For the pain points,
we unpack and unravel
some of the limiting beliefs that clients might have.

I principally work
with creatives, strategists, and marketing folks
from around the world.

Interestingly,
a lot of the issues and themes are similar,
all be it on a very personal basis.

Time is spent with clients
toggling between their vision and pain points.
To allow them to sit,
recognise and address
these pain points specifically.

Equally it is an opportunity to encourage them
to thrive in their pursuit
of their goal or vision.

To their question, "*Why?*",
the response should be '*Why not?*'

And if they try some time,
it not only helps people
to get what they need,
they'll get what they deserve too.

Titles Aren't Important

I've gone from Brand Builder to Kindness Avenger.
Manager, Director,
Vice President,
Chief Marketing Officer, Founder.

Wait – that's nonsense.

I haven't 'gone' anywhere,
I've always been me.
It's just taken me awhile
to find my voice
and the 'thing' that gets me up in the morning.

Your title isn't you.
It doesn't define you.
(Nor should it.)
You define 'you.'
And whoever you are,
go celebrate *you* today.

A Reason To Be

Okay, talking about eulogies
might be a little unexpected
in a book about work,
so please bear with me.
I experienced two close family bereavements
within the space of 18 days.
It impacted my family in many ways,
across the generations:
siblings, cousins, aunts, uncles, children, grandchildren.

Everyone had their story to tell,
their relationship
with those loved ones,
who had passed away.
The overwhelming take-away,
was the reminder that life is short.

It is precious.
And special.
It is not something
we should ever assume

or take for granted.
One of those who passed,
my cousin Nick,
was just five years older than me.
Five years.

I have spent much of my professional career
working for some amazing brands,
with amazing people.
The focus of that work
has been very much about
finding the meaning,
that dreaded word 'purpose'
for those brands,
their existence in the world.
Their contribution.
The value that they bring.
The sad events of the past months
have made me remind myself
of my own purpose.
My 'why'.

It made me reflect on,
when it is my turn
to shuffle off this mortal coil,
what people will say about me
and my contribution to the world.
At the heart of what I now do as a coach,
is my desire
to enable people to be seen, heard, and valued at work.

If somewhere in the opening lines of my eulogy,
amidst the sadness,
somebody says:
"Neil enabled people to be seen, heard and valued"
then my mission,
my purpose,
and my work will be complete.

So, what is your purpose?
Your true purpose?
We spend approximately
90,000 hours at work in our lifetimes.

Starting today,
roughly calculate
how many of those hours you have left.
Think about how you feel.
Are you fulfilling your true purpose?
Are you bringing joy and kindness
to everything you do at work?
And beyond all the clichés and memes,
in all honesty,
Are you truly living your best life?

So,
what are you going to do
with your hours?

Your Personal Board Of Directors

Think of a handful of people,
say four or five
who you truly click with
at a higher level,
who give great energy,
who 'get' you.
You appreciate
their company,
their counsel,
their opinion.
They'll tell it to you straight,
especially things
you might not want to hear.

Invest in these people.
They are your personal board of directors.
Treat yourself
like a company.
You are the best asset
for that company (you).

These people
can come from all parts of your life.
It doesn't have to be the obvious ones.
The important thing
is they speak their truth authentically.

They celebrate your vulnerability.
And they love you
for being you.

That's what counts.

Be Present. Now

Many years ago,
a good friend of mine
shared some wise words
that I've frequently come back to:
'Life is a bad hand played well.'

In this context
I've always valued
gratitude as a choice.
It's about being open-minded,
open-hearted.

Shifting
your expectations and mindset.
This takes work.
It takes practice.
However, you can take steps
to start and end your day,
with the right mindset.

My invitation to you is this.

Before you go to sleep at night,
before you turn out the light
or close your eyes.,
take a moment for yourself.
To breathe deeply,
maybe smile to yourself.

Think of three things
that you are grateful for,
things that may have happened in your day.
These could be small moments,
gestures or thoughts.

Repeat the same exercise
when you wake up in the morning.

Open your eyes.

Think of three things that you are grateful for.
Or three things
that you are grateful for,
that might be happening today.

Try and maintain these thoughts,
this feeling,
for as long as possible.

Stay in that higher frequency.
Avoid checking your phone
for as long as possible.

Nothing is more of a buzz kill
than diving
into social media,
news headlines,
or emails.

Be in control.
Maintain that feeling of gratitude
for as long as you're able.
For one minute, five minutes, an hour.

The more you practice,
the more you will embrace
a mindset of gratitude.

It'll really set you up for the day.
And help you appreciate
what matters to you,
what you're grateful for.

Win the morning, win the day.

It's Important. Go Deeper

Here's the quiet part loud.

People rarely just leave jobs for more money elsewhere.
No, they leave because
they feel unheard,
unappreciated
for their work.

When was the last time
you had a proper conversation
with individuals in your team?

Not a *'How are you?'*
'Great, thanks' conversation.

I'm suggesting a proper talk,
where you make time to understand
what is actually going on in their lives,
what is important to them right now.
It could be the most important conversation you have this week.

Tick, Tick, Tock

Momentum doesn't always mean moving.

Take time each day to think.
Reflect.
To just be.

It might not feel much,
or like you are making a difference.

Remember
even at a red stop light,
a car's engine is still ticking over.

Kindness. It's Not A Random Thing

Let's take a moment
to celebrate the power of kindness.
To highlight the incredible impact that it has.

On ourselves,
the people around us,
at work,
in our communities,
and the world we all share and live in.

All too often kindness
is somehow perceived as 'random'
or soft, when it's not.

It's also not a logo
on a T-shirt or tote bag.
(Although that helps keep the message out there for all to see.)

No, kindness isn't random.
Kindness is an action.
It's a mindset and a choice,
and it starts with you.

So be intentional.

Do it with an open heart,
not because you want something in return.

Do it for the cause not the applause.

Make a choice.
There's nothing random about it.

Practice *Actionable Kindness* ™ every day.

The 80/20 Rule

We can't all be good at everything.
(Sorry, spoiler alert but it's true.)

Each of us has special gifts,
talents that are unique to us.

It could be in the way
we think or communicate,
what we're able to make or create.

An ability with numbers
or languages.
There are many variations.

Companies are little ecosystems
made-up of individuals
that all contribute,
hopefully,
to a common goal or purpose.

In our own ways
we all have a part to play,
we all have something
that we contribute.

As a percentage
we should look at things as the 80/20 rule.
Meaning there's probably 80% of things
that we do either well,
very well or exceed at.

Then there's probably 20% of things
that we're either okay,
average,
or just not good at.
That's okay.

Through coaching conversations over the years,
my observation is that
many of us
tend to dwell on the 20%.

The things we wished we did better,
could do better,
or would like to improve on.

As a coach,
I often hear people
putting themselves down
about the things that they can't do.

I often ask people,
"What about the 80%?
The things that you can do,
or you recognise in yourself
that you are good at?
Or importantly that others
see that skill or talent in you?"

This usually creates an 'Aha' moment,
when people recognise,
'Actually yes, I am good at X
or I do get recognised for Y.'

This little exercise
gives people a lift,
a boost of confidence,
to recognise the place
where they should be focusing
their energy and efforts.

Now this might sound
like a contradiction,
however, I'm also a big advocate of learning.

Of trying something new.
For developing skills.

I also acknowledge
that if you have a lack of a skill,
that is a requirement for a particular job,
that is not a justification
for looking the other way.

Often men will look
at a potential job description
and feel confident
that they have the ability
to do 80% of what is being asked,
whilst women feel that having 'only' 80% percent is not enough.

What's a quick way of establishing your own 80/20?

Read through your job description.
Put it to one side.

Now write down in your own words,
what you actually do.

Then write down five things
that you feel that you are good
or excellent at.
(everyone has this).

Then ask a good friend,
family member,
or co-worker the same question:
"What are five things that I'm good at?"

See how much of the two lists
tally and overlap.
Within this list
could be lurking your superpower.

Go explore your 80% today.

The Power Of The Pause

How often do you take time for yourself on a daily basis?

It starts with a shift in mindset.
Of letting go
of things you can't control,
and reflecting on things
you can control.

Start moving to observe
the small things
like warmth, light,
a cup or a drink.

The goal is to bring your attention
to the now.
To today.
To the space you are in and
the simple things around you.

Carving out small moments in our day
to stop and pause is essential.
It's a moment to reflect,
to breathe,
to ground ourselves.

It needn't be long.
The important thing is
we take back control of ourselves.

Even for a few minutes,
to appreciate the small things.

Before we jump back
onto the merry-go-round of life today.

Knowing

Some people
are predictably unpredictable.

As a good friend I worked with in advertising
would regularly tell me:
'Never interrupt a man making a complete ass of himself.'

Monday Muse

Monday.
It's a New Moon.
A chance to start over,
a new cycle, new growth.

So how do you want to spend
the time that you are awake?
Five days working,
and then two days off,
just to recover?

Or do you see your life
as seven days
in each week,
365 days
in each year?
It is not about a 'work-life' balance.
It's about finding 'life-life' harmony.

Which are you choosing today?
'Work-life' or 'life-life'?

P.S. I know Monday morning is hectic,
and everyone's too busy
to be answering big 'life' questions,
but that's kind of my point.

There's Enough Time. Just Don't Waste It

I don't know Warren Buffett,
but I like some of his observations.

He often states that financially,
he is pretty much able to buy anything
that he would want.

However, he recognizes the one thing
that he cannot buy is time.

I encourage you to put a 'ring fence'
around the things
that are really important to you.

Arguably, time
is one of the most precious
commodities we have in life.
(And business.)

Never give away your time.
We have enough.
Just don't waste it.

Everyday Kindness And Kindness Every Day

Our levels of anxiety are running high.
Levels of doubt,
levels of uncertainty;
Social, political, environmental -
the list goes on.

It means that the days are long,

The weeks are long,
the months are long,
and the year?
Well, what year is it right now, anyway?

However, I've always been inspired
by a tapestry
that hung in my grandmother's house.
The words consistently resonate with me.

"I shall pass through this world but once.
Any good things therefore I can do,
or any kindness that I can show,
let me do it now,
For I shall not pass this way again."

It was written at a time
when being present,
being in the now,
wasn't the trendy thing to say.
However, it's as true today
as it's always been.

Think about where you are,
on any given moment,
on any given day.

Just say to yourself,
"What can I give,
or share in this moment,
a positive act or thought,
some kind of actionable kindness?"

You can't do better than that.
That minute has gone,
the next one is coming.
Just be present.

Be in the now,
do the best that you can.
Be as kind, as thoughtful
as is right and appropriate,
in that moment.

And that's all any of us can do.

Love Bomb

Kindness is like love.
Nobody owns it.
But everybody can benefit from it.

And like love, it starts with yourself.
How are you going to give yourself
a bit of space and grace today?

Get It Done

There are only two reasons why things do not get done.

1. You don't want to do it.
2. You don't know how to do it.

The 'how' part can be really broad.
It can be time, resources, budget.
It's usually a pretty good place to start,
when trying to unpack
how to do something.

However next time you say
"I don't want to do it",
ask yourself an honest question.

Is it that you truly don't want to do it -
out of principle,
or it conflicts with your values,
that kind of thing?

Or is it that truthfully,
you don't know how to do it?

Asking the question 'how' to do something,
is another way of saying, *"I need help."*

Let's normalise the practice of asking for help.
Too often at work
there is a stigma attached to it.
It's seen as a weakness.

Truth is, we can't know the answer to everything.
We shouldn't always be
the smartest person in the room.
There's always an opportunity to learn.

'Can you help me?'

Sleep On It

Sometimes
it's just not your day.
In life, at work.

A sequence of events
beyond our control.

Things just don't go our way.
It happens.

If this is you today,
then make a decision.

Draw a line under today.
Instead of spiralling,
racking your brain
into the night,
or looking at the world
through
the bottom of a glass,

make a choice.
Go to bed.

And preferably
earlier
than you normally do.

Disconnect from devices.
Take a warm shower.
Get into bed.
Switch out the light.

Feel confident
that you have made
one positive choice
for yourself today.

The extra rest,
recovery
and sleep
will leave you charged.
Re-energized.

The problem or situation
may still be there
in the morning.

However,
you will be able to tackle it
with fresh eyes,
a fresh mind.

Too often
when confronted
by so many questions,
sleep is the answer.

Stand Tall

People can only walk all over you,
if you're lying down.

Your Kindness Quota

When you look back,
what will your kindness quota look like?

How will your words, deeds,
and actions be remembered?

With friends and family?
In your community?

What about at work?

We spend a significant amount
of our waking hours at work;
why shouldn't we
be remembered
for kindness in the workplace?

Let's start today.

You Can Rely On Someone To Let You Down

I have a business contact,
let's call them 'Bob.'
(Not their real name, I don't think I know anyone called
Bob.)

We've spoken about working together
on several occasions,
and collaborating on projects.

I've made introductions to Bob,
without acknowledgement.

I've shared concepts and ideas,
without recognition.

We've passed each other
whilst out and about grabbing coffee.
"Hey, we should catch up, I'll be in touch." says Bob.
Yet I get nothing back in return,
and that can feel frustrating.

It's taken me a while to reconcile,
that it's not me.
I've now realized that Bob
is someone I can rely on to let me down.

Having good people around is so important;
to take counsel from,
to support you,
to help shine the light on you and your path ahead.
When you're trying to identify your superpowers,
you need to pick and choose
the opinions you value.

You don't have to agree
with everything someone says.
You can acknowledge it,
but you don't have to accept it.

You know your true value and self-worth.
And you can thank the Bobs of the world for that.

Innovation Without Recrimination

When brands move too fast,
there's often a lack of clarity.
Speed without clarity
is the root of major inefficiencies
within organizations
large or small.

How we focus,
how we prioritize and do our tasks,
becomes easier if we are all aligned
to the common goal for that week, month, year.
Kindness, clarity and trust are key to achieving this.
Clarity of the plan and the process.
Trust in one another.

And kindness
to create a calm, secure environment
that supports innovation,
collaboration,
experimentation without recrimination.
That's when the magic truly happens.

Thought For The Weekend

Are you still stuck in the same routine,
waiting for Friday?

Nothing is going to change,
unless you take a step.
Yes, just one step in a different direction.

Use this weekend
to start to build the life you want,
instead of trying to
escape the life you have.
We only get one.
Make it a good one.

Winning Combination

When people feel secure,
appreciated,
they perform better.

Research has shown
that a kind, calm,
supportive environment
reduces anxiety,
improves morale,
increases productivity.

If someone feels
like you've got their back,
they are more likely
to go the extra mile,
to take risks to try something new.

As the saying goes,
"Nobody ever had a good idea whilst being chased by a tiger."

Kindness and calmness win every time.

Your Move

It really doesn't matter
where you are in life.
The great thing about life is,
it is your next move that counts.

No matter where you are.
You could change your life,
if you want to.
It is your next decision that matters.

In Your Head

Don’t let ‘perfect’ get in the way of ‘good.’

Start Small. Win Big

Join the dots
and your people feel connected.
Provide simplicity
and clarity for their contribution
to their daily tasks,
to the overall purpose of the company.
Close the gap
and they feel empowered.
Empowered to achieve their ambitions,
to tackle their limiting beliefs and pain points.

Watch your people grow
in an environment
that inspires
trust,
loyalty,
collaboration,
innovation,
creativity.
It's achievable

by taking small steps each day:

Instilling a culture of *kindness*,
and an appreciation of *gratitude;*
being able to acknowledge
the small things
that make a difference
to one another;
sharpening
your individual
and team's skills
to be able to pivot
when needed.

Baking in
an inherent sense of *resilience*
and 'can-do' attitude,
that we're all in this together,
no matter what.

It's important
that we keep going
and don't give up.
And finally,
encourage a mindset of *momentum:*

Appreciating
the power to pause,
then accelerate.

Taking The First Step

Early on in my career,
a chance conversation
gave me a break,
and I've never forgotten that.

It was a previously unseen opportunity,
one that needed to be explored
with a mix
of curiosity and confidence.

It probably wasn't called
networking
or coaching back then.

However,
opportunities happen
when people step forwards
and engage with one another
with an open mind.

Today my work revolves
around enabling people
to be seen, heard and valued.
Same principle, different execution.
Shining the light on people.
Giving them a moment
to reflect,
to recognize their true potential.

Something that is already within them.
They just need to take a deep breath,
say the words
or take that first step forwards.
My focus is on inspiring
the next generation of leaders.

To be their best.
To create a legacy mindset.
To inspire a groundswell of positivity in business.

Be known
as that *kindness accelerator,*
the *curious disruptor,*
or the *bold advocate* in your company.
It all starts with yourself.

When

If you're not going to do it when you're alive,
when are you going to do it?

Two Ears, One Mouth

Be cautious of people
who listen,
to just reply
with their opinion,
rather than listening
to understand
someone else's.

The Name Game

Here's why I named
my coaching consultancy Mercury Jam.

Mercury is a liquid metal,
affected by heat,
constantly in motion.
It changes shape,
shifts with speed.

Jam can be sweet,
and sticky,
with tasty ingredients.

It can mean just *jammin'*
and doing your thing.

Mercury Jam
is about the combination
of you moving
with speed at work,

and how you can combine it
with the most important
ingredients
of your daily life.

Those little moments of joy,
that really make the difference,
that stand out.
That makes you, '*you*'.
That's *your* Mercury Jam.

If you have things
that bring you daily joy
post them on social media using
#mercury_jam_coaching
I'd love to feature them on my page.

Thought For The Day

Aim for action not perfection.

Chapter 3.

Make Work Better

"Don't ask us to attend 'cos we're not all there.
Oh, don't pretend 'cos I don't care.
I don't believe illusions 'cos too much is real.
So, stop your cheap comment 'cos we know what we feel"

Sex Pistols - "Pretty Vacant"

The sentiment behind this chapter
is a little spicy.
We are at a point in time
where companies need to 'adapt or die.'

Punk was a moment,
before it became a movement.
People are having a moment.
A punk moment.

They have had enough
of not being appreciated or valued,
their contribution unrecognised.

You can dress it up all you want as
the 'Great Resignation,' 'Great Reshuffle,'
or 'Quiet Quitting.'

We need change,
not another label to describe the problem.
There is an explosion of emotion.
There is an individual 'can-do' attitude at odds with
corporate culture.
There is a willingness to make a difference,
to make a change.

A groundswell of individual activism not in the streets,
but in offices, at kitchen tables, on zoom calls.
(Camera on – optional.)

The pandemic was the catalyst.
It was the final spark
to the powder keg of discontent,
of human dissatisfaction.

And we're not going to take it anymore.
The façade, the pretence, the illusion is done.

No more,
don't pretend,
because we don't care.

And if you think that we're just all out to lunch,
truth is we're not actually coming back.

This is the new reality.
This is a watershed moment
to come together.

To do things differently.
It's on everyone to contribute,
to take notice, to play their part.

If you can't be sincere,
if you can't value
the people who work for you,
then don't ask us to attend,
'cos we're not all there.

Action And Impact

Kindness
means different things to different people.
However, it has the impact
of moving people in similar ways.

My definition of kindness
is enabling people to be seen,
to be heard,
to be valued.

What's your definition?
What does kindness mean to you?

Not Listening To Reply. Listening To Learn

Many years ago,
my son came home from school,
slightly perturbed.
His class had been asked what their fathers did for work,
and he didn't know.

"Daddy?" replied his mother with a dry smile,
"Daddy just talks for a living."

At the time it was kind of true,
as I was working in global advertising for Lenovo in the US.

Fast forward 10 years,
I'm still talking for a living.
Importantly, as a Business Coach and People Strategist,
I'm listening more.

Really listening.

I'm listening to my clients
to understand
their pain points and limiting beliefs.

Listening to what excites them,
what their passions,
hopes and aspirations are.

My goal for them
is to reach
their true potential,
by enabling them to *be seen, heard, and valued.*
To become the kind of leaders
that people
genuinely want to follow.

Yes,
we can do this
by talking,
but we all need

to listen more as well.

Not listening
just to reply.

Listening
to truly understand
one another.

Energy Management vs Time Management

The traditional working week,
Monday to Friday,
9 to 5 is dead.
But we still need to tackle prioritisation,
to prevent getting overwhelmed
and underperforming.
So how do we 'juggle the struggle'?

By looking at the patterns of our energy levels
during the day.

Working From Home
meant we had to adapt
to different rhythms and routines.
For some, they may be more productive
or have more energy
at the beginning of the day,
with a dip in the afternoon.

Others may wish to leave
more admin-based tasks
or responses to the evening.
Or it could be in steady blocks
during the day
with regular breaks.

It's a mindset, to enable
people to prioritize
their personal and professional lives,
into one succinct action plan.

In time it enhances
well-being and productivity,
and enables greater focus and impact.

Check In

What are some of the key ingredients
of top performing teams?

First - Trust and connection.
It can make the difference
between a good team
and a truly great one.

Second - Getting comfortable being open,
feeling vulnerable,
is a key part in this too.

Thirdly - productivity and efficiency;
everyone facing the same way
metaphorically.

Yet do we make the most of the time
we spend together at work?
Let's be honest,
meetings are mostly a waste of time.

Lack of an agenda,
no focus,
often the wrong combination of people.
("Why am I here?")

There's a simple
yet effective practice
that is rocket fuel for teams.
A game changer.

Allowing time for participants
to check into a meeting
increases focus and attention,
leading to a more
productive conversation.

There are two questions that are used
to check-in at the beginning of each successful meeting.
(For example, a status meeting with the team.)

1. "How are you doing today?"
Meaning not generally, not overall,
but today, here personally, in this moment.

2. "What would keep you from being present right here,
right now?
Are there any distractions large or small,
that would prevent you from giving your full attention? "

This could be:
A disagreement with a family member this morning;
what to add to your grocery list;
there's an unpaid bill;
you have a big presentation coming up soon.

By giving the time for each participant
to express how they are feeling,
you enable that group of individuals
to be focused and engaged
on the task at hand.

It grounds them in the moment,
and puts aside thoughts or distractions.

The set up and process is important.

Each participant is invited
to respond to the questions,
in the most open and authentic way
that they feel able to
in that moment.

The others listen quietly
and respectfully.

They do not add,
they do not comment.

If someone is struggling,
they do not reach out
(and this is with good intent.)

After answering the questions,
the respondent says
"check" or "I'm done."
The other members of the group
respond by acknowledging,
"Thank you for sharing."

The order that people speak in
is completely arbitrary.
It's intentionally non-hierarchical.
It's an opportunity for everyone
to express how they feel.

Sometimes people are feeling
energised and positive,
other times feeling low.
This is an opportunity to understand
where everybody's head is at
on any given day,
in the moment.

A chance to check the temperature,
to read the room.
It also allows every member of the team,
whether junior or senior,
to have their voice heard.

This encourages and increases
people's willingness to speak up.

I have witnessed on many occasions
meetings where people arrive and depart
as quietly as a mouse.

They may have an idea,
or a contribution to share.
However, there is a reluctance to speak up
or raise their hand
when the terms of participation
have not been explained.
I acknowledge that there are
differing ways of doing business,

that different business cultures
place more attention
on hierarchy than others.

However, the power of the 'Check In'
should not be underestimated.

Many years ago,
there was a junior team member
who was experiencing
some personal challenges
outside of work.
The impact of their words still resonates with me today.
In response to the question,
"How are you doing today?"
they replied, *"This Check In is the one place that I can
feel and be myself right now."*
Now, back to the process.

It takes time to build this culture to 'Check In'
within a team or department,
or ideally across an organisation.
It requires the individual leading the meeting
to be highly tuned in,
to the frequency,
the vibration of that group.

It calls upon us to use our listening skills,
observing
non-verbal cues and communication,
more so than our verbal skills.
However, by investing time in your people,
the impact can be transformational.

It truly enables them
to be seen, heard, and valued.

Breathing Is The Smart Choice

Special offer:
'Personal investment opportunity,
make hundreds an hour.'

On average,
we breathe sixteen times a minute.
That's nine hundred and sixty times an hour

Use your time wisely.
Finance your heart first.
The rest of you will profit in time.

Take the moments to just be,
just breathe.
Invest in yourself a bit.

Bird On A Branch

Have you ever watched a bird
sitting on a branch in the wind?

Despite the wind,
the bird seems secure
as the branch sways back and forth,
up and down.
It appears confident,
unruffled.

Why is this?
It holds this presence
and demeanour
in the knowledge
that even if the branch
snaps and drops,
the bird's wings
will lift it up to fly to safety.

We should endevour
to create a similar environment
of psychological safety at work.

Even if the metaphorical branch breaks,
we should feel confident
in the belief
that we will fly,
not fall.

Thought For The Day

Shifting your perspectives
by just a few degrees,
can make the difference
between looking
at a wall,
and looking
out of a window.

Sailing Into Winds

About a year ago,
my sister sent me a card
as I was going through a tough time.
I was in the 'eye of the storm.'

Many things were in transition.
COVID was raging, we were in lockdown.
I was building my business and client-base,
whilst navigating divorce,
and my family were relocating far away.

Yet this simple message really resonated:
"We cannot direct the wind, but we can adjust the sails."
There are forces in the universe
which are bigger and greater than us,
like the wind.

We can't necessarily influence
or change them.
Instead, we go with the flow.

What we can do
is work with the wind,
to set our own personal sails in a direction
so that we leverage
the power of the wind to drive us forward,
to keep some momentum.
When things seem tough,
or out of your control,
look at where your own sails are
on your own 'personal little boat.'

I often look at this card
and remember that it all starts
with being kind to yourself.

Recognizing that, '*indeed this thing shall pass*'
and to complete the sailing analogy,
we can ride out the storm
and sail into calmer waters.

Practice everyday kindness,
and kindness every day.

Always Have One Thought To Share

If you're an introvert
or even an ambivert,
always prepare for a meeting
by having one thought
you would like to share in the conversation.

Listen,
read the room.
Find your moment.
Deliver your thought.

A simple tip to capture the attention
is to repeat
the last thing that somebody says,
and then build on it,
with your own thought.

For example:
"So, Jenny, what I'm hearing
is that we will focus on three things for the next quarter."

"To build on that, I have been thinking
about how we can bring
more innovation to our products
at an earlier stage of development."

By doing that you have built a bridge
and inserted your thoughts,
opinion,
or contribution
into the conversation seamlessly.

Practice this at home or with friends and family.
Gradually your confidence
and competence will increase.
You feel part of the conversation.
Engaged in the process.

I introduced this technique
to a co-worker many years ago,
when they were relatively new to the team.
They were full of great ideas

however, the environment
was not conducive
to receive their voice.

Fast forward.
That same co-worker
has used this technique
throughout the course
of their career.

They have carved out a niche for themselves
as a thoughtful and insightful contributor.

They now lead the Design Department,
as Vice President
for a multi-billion-dollar company.

Start small.
Practice.
Repeat.
And see where your ideas will take you.

Boredom Is Freedom

Find time to do nothing this weekend.
Literally.
Be bored, be still, be restless.
It's good to let your mind
just wonder.

Being busy
for busy's sake
won't get you far.
You need downtime to be productive.

Put down that device.
Don't make plans
that aren't 100% essential.

Just be.
Just be bored.

Something to think about.
Or not.

Ten Red Balloons

We have a finite capacity
to concentrate
and achieve things,
in any moment,
on any given day.

There's a habit of writing
long to-do lists,
stuffed full of all manner of tasks,
large and small.

We get overwhelmed.
And stuck.
Next time this happens,
try this visualisation technique.

Imagine each task you have
is a red balloon.

The balloons are filled with helium,
bobbing about,
attached with a piece of string.

Some days we collect more balloons
than we can handle.
The balloons knock into one another.
They make that annoying squeaky balloon sound.

The strings get twisted,
and we get frustrated
and lose focus.

Here's the thing.
You can only keep
a maximum
of three balloons
in your hand,
ideally less.

Ask yourself:
"Which balloon is my priority right here, right now?"
"Which ones will I need to let go of today?"
The act of letting go
can be challenging.
At first, you wrestle with your conscience
for which is the priority.

Through repeated practice
this exercise becomes easier.
Your day becomes more fluid and seamless.

It is a simple exercise,
which is both liberating
and empowering at the same time.

Give it a whirl.
If you don't like red balloons
choose a different colour.

The important thing is that you just try.

Is The Future More Uncertain?

Question:
Is the future more uncertain today,
than say two or three years ago?

Answer:
Conceptually the answer is 'No.'

It is the uncertainty
that triggers anxiety.
As humans
we can speculate
what the future might be.
For sure, we can do vision exercises
and manifestations.

To achieve this,
we first need to connect with ourselves.
To manage expectations,
to bring ourselves
back into the present.

It's a way to maintain focus,
momentum,
and productivity.

When so many of us
are running on fumes
right now,
it's essential
to build moments
in our day to pause.

To refocus,
to be in the now.

Strategically
it ensures we are focusing
on the priority
at that moment.
Ironically,
understanding the power of pausing

is a key part
of maintaining momentum.

Especially when
we are challenged
to pivot
so frequently these days.

Outlook

Be prepared for the rain,
be prepared for sunshine.

There's no such thing as good weather or bad weather.

It's all down to your approach to it.
Same goes for work.

Book A Break On A Break

The best time to book a break or vacation
is when you're on a break or vacation.
Read that again.
On vacation we are relaxed (hopefully!)
Physically and mentally in a good place.
We are focusing on ourselves,
our family, friends or loved ones.

We're enjoying that time,
maybe just relaxing
or being active.
This is what we live for,
this sense of being.
Being at one.
Just being alive.
Not stuck in the grind.
Not on Zoom calls.
The endless cycle of meetings and reports.
That's not why we're alive.

Trying to schedule time off
when you're at work
and in the weeds,
is not productive.

You will always find a reason not to go.

What's more important?
A meeting
or your well-being.
(And by the way you're legally entitled to take time off
without the guilt trip.)

We can work hard.
We can be loyal to our company.
To our team.

However,
we should be loyal to ourselves first,
put our needs front and centre.
So next time you're on a break or vacation,
try it.

Look at your calendar,
and pencil the time off.

You won't look back.

Compete, Peacefully

When you have a calm,
supportive working environment,
you are creating a space
where everybody knows the expectations.
It's then understood that it's okay to ask questions,
to share thoughts
and different points of views,
and challenging them is encouraged.

It's just human nature.
When teams know how to connect
and communicate with one another,
this enables them to compete peacefully.

It creates spaces for curiosity.
Which in turn increases interaction,
productivity and harmony.

And that's the role that kindness plays.
It's the glue that brings it all together.

Thought For The Weekend

There's one thing
more precious than our time,
and that's who we spend it with.

Think about that again on Monday morning.

We only get one life.
Make it a good one.

Life After Burnout

There is life after burnout.
How do I know this?

In the late '90s,
I experienced a significant burnout.
Triggering a bout of depression.
It lasted almost twelve months.

I had to step away from a job that I loved,
in a company I loved.
A place where I was starting to get traction,
from a career point of view.
The impact of the burnout
ended the relationship I was in at the time.
I almost lost my apartment in London,
and things began to spiral.
And not in a good way.

What I would say is
that sometimes, things need to fall apart

and unravel,
to understand
where you're truly meant to be in life.
It puts things in perspective.

The majority of, quote, 'my success',
in terms of achievements and experience,
both personal and professional,
has come after my burnout.

Burnout is a dark place.
However, it's also a chance to recalibrate.
To re-evaluate
what's important to you,
and your life.

I now take steps to self-care,
to see the signs that trigger negative energy
and contribute to the early phases of burnout.

I share these learnings with others.
I encourage the principles
of *kindness, gratitude, resilience* and *momentum*.
To help people 'juggle the struggle' of finding
balance and harmony
with their life and work.

My circumstances that contributed
to the original burnout
may be different from others,
although it was definitely work related.

However, the message
and the sentiment are the same.

There is hope.

There are new beginnings.
Day always follows night.
Light follows dark.

And as hard as it is to say,
it takes time to believe in yourself again,
I know, but you will.

What's something positive
that you've experienced post-burnout?

Speaking up and sharing
might help someone who's having a tough time today.

Thought For The Day

Start small.
Start simple.
Just start.

Be Known For Something

Be known as that kindness accelerator,
the curious disruptor,
or the bold advocate
in your company.
It all starts with yourself.

Give The Gift Of Listening

Struggling for a last-minute gift idea
for a birthday,
or the holidays?
Or do you just want to recognise someone's contribution?

Enabling someone
to feel seen, heard and valued
is more important than ever.

And it starts with listening.
Really listening,
Like
'full attention-one-on-one-no-interruptions-no-phone-pinging'
listening.

Why not offer an hour of free listening time
to a co-worker,
friend or family member?

Truly engage with them
through listening
by asking thoughtful,
curious,
encouraging questions.

(Gentle reminder: it's their gift, so it's about them not you.)

The memory and impact
will last longer
than any gift voucher
or coffee card.

To-Do's vs To-Don'ts

Q: Do you know the best way to shorten your to-do lists?
A: Put fewer things on them.
Okay, it might sound flippant.
However, here's a couple of considerations.

If there's something
that can take 60 seconds or less,
just do it.

Don't even put it on a list.
We need to practice a sense of scale
when creating to-do lists.

Setting our intentions.
Tackling the big rocks first.
And we can't do that
if we are giving
the same amount
of (head) space
on the page,

to following up
on quick admin emails.

Secondly,
our brains only have
the capabilities to achieve
two or three sizable tasks in one day.

After that our attention to detail,
focus and concentration
starts to fall away.

It is also recommended
to start the day
with the hardest
or most complex challenge.

For most people,
this is when our minds
are most receptive

and attuned to tackling these challenges.
For example,
I often review my to-do list
for the coming day
at the end of the previous one.

That way I wake up
knowing the specific thing
that I need to be focusing on.

This is the mindset
that I begin the day with,
avoiding getting distracted
by emails, admin and social media.

But not coffee.
Coffee is good way to start my day.

Be Seen

Have you had a conversation with someone
that left you feeling
more confident,
more at peace,
more energized?
What was it that made the difference?

They likely did something
that most people
strongly desire from others.

They made you feel seen.

Feeling 'seen' means
feeling known,
heard,
understood.
It means that someone
not only
pays attention to you,

but also ‘gets’ you,
and gets where you are coming from.

People with the gift of seeing others
have a special energy.

Who doesn’t want to be around someone
who genuinely cares?
That cares enough to truly listen,
to pay attention.
To ask thoughtful questions.

To be curious
about you and your well-being.

Let’s all be people that really see others.
Make a point to
be present,
pay attention,
to be in the moment.

It puts positive energy
back into the universe.

And we all need
positive energy right now.

Go All The Way

OOO
There's a clue in there.
Out Of Office.
As in out, away, not there, unavailable.

It's not OOOBIBCETAD
'Out Of Office But I'll Be Checking Emails Twice A Day.'

Or OOOBCMIYHQ
'Out Of Office But Call Me If You Have Questions.'

When you go on vacation
be kind to yourself,
your peers,
your line managers.
Unplug.
Disconnect.
Delete or hide those apps.

Spend time with yourself.
Your friends.
Your loved ones.
With nature.
Be kind.
Be truly out of the office.

Peeling The Onion

It's important to be ourselves,
at all times.
Including the workplace.
To show up
with our true identity and values.
To shine a light
on our true potential.
To give ourselves permission
to have doubts and off-days.
After all,
'It's okay not to be okay.'
and to show emotions.
It's powerful to acknowledge
'I don't know' as a leader.

You don't have to be the smartest person
in the room all the time.
Not having the answer
can help open up the conversation.
It allows us to be human,

to be 'more like you' in the workplace.
So, go on a journey.

Peel the onion.

Slowly reveal your true self.
There should be no distinction
in how you show up at work
or outside of work.

Show your whole self,
your true self,
your *me* self.

Why?

Teams want leaders they can believe in.
Leaders who are human and fallible.
Who lead with conviction,
and yet are humble enough

to ask questions and take counsel.
As an individual or as a leader
you will be more satisfied
in the work that you do,
and your contribution to it,
by being true to you.

Comfort vs Progress

Do you know about the two-minute rule?

Research has shown
that when trying something new,
focusing on the first two minutes
is the decisive time in our brain
to keep going, or give up too quickly.
This mental tension is critical
when we are trying a new routine
or learning a new skill.

For example,
we want to wake up earlier
or go to the gym (or both.)

Often it is the psychological act of
getting up,
getting off the couch,
getting out of bed,
that can be the challenging part.
Those two minutes

are the battleground
between comfort and progress.

We literally need to make ourselves
feel uncomfortable
and dwell in that moment,
for us to make progress.

Breaking it down into those two-minute segments
is a simple and effective way
to start something new.

Building that muscle memory
helps in those first moments,
to be comfortable being uncomfortable.

It then allows us
to push on through
to the next level
and the next challenge.

Kindness As The Catalyst

In a recent Financial Times survey,
only 21% of people said that they felt engaged at work.
Meaning 79%,
or more than 3/4 of people,
are feeling unfulfilled,
and not engaged in their job.

That's a wasted opportunity.
Of lives, talent, resource,
ideas, innovation, connection.
All underutilized and idling away.

And behind the statistics
let's not fool ourselves
by labeling them employees.
They are people,
humans,
just like you and me.

Humans who are not engaged,

and aren't living up to their best,
to their full potential.
That's got to be wrong, right?

There must be a better way.
Surely the playbook is out there,
with all this talk of values, culture and purpose?

To be fair, there are some good companies
'walking the walk and talking the talk.'
So, what's an alternative?
In my opinion, kindness is the catalyst.

It is the glue,
that combines strategy, people and outcomes.
And to all the haters and cynics out there,
why not give it a whirl?

79% of people might agree too.

Seeing Things Differently

Sometimes we should pause
from our work journey and reflect.

You're trying to pivot to a new role,
to recalibrate what's next,
or maybe get back into the game.

Reaching out to your network.
Trying to get your foot in the door.
Hopeful of an introduction, conversation or interview.

This is challenging.
It takes a lot of energy.
Our confidence can take a knock too.

Especially if you were not getting a response
from the right people.
Or unwanted attention
from the wrong people.

It pays to keep a tally
on how many of our 90,000 hours
we have left,
and make a choice.

If the corporate world doesn't deliver,
and is not giving you what you want,
it is up to you to recognise your experience,
your self-worth and value,
and create your own path forwards.

Do your own thing.
Scary?
Sure.

It just takes one step at a time.

Meeting Hygiene

"Well, that was a waste of time."

How many times have you said that,
or heard that
about a particular meeting?
Have you ever stopped
to consider
why the meeting happened
in the first place?
Time is something that we cannot buy.

Sure, we put a perceived value to it
in terms of how much
somebody is worth per hour,
what their hourly rate might be.

In all honesty,
that is purely subjective.
Time marches on;
we'll never get that time back.

Similarly,
the time it took you
to read this last sentence
will never be repeated.

So, I guess I better get to the point.

Treat meetings like it's your own money you're spending.

If it's your money,
wouldn't you want to make sure
you have the right people
in the room or on the call?
It might be the 'company's money' per se
but the company
still doesn't own that time.
Nobody does.

Let’s do a quick calculation for a one-hour meeting

Ten people attend a meeting.

Based on imaginary hourly rates
2 people cost €200 per hour,
3 cost €150,
5 cost €75 per hour.
Therefore, the cost of the one-hour meeting is €1,225.

Would you spend €1,225
on something
that had no purpose,
no agenda,
no clear input
or output,
no real value?

And yet we accept this as normal practice
hour after hour, day after day.
Would you throw away
that time and money?
Could you afford to do that?

Unlikely.

Yet we do it every day at work.
There's enough time,
just don't waste it.

Be More You. Money Is Energy

I'm a big fan of Marvin Gaye.
I love his music,
but also the stories of his life.

In 1978 he owed his ex-wife Anna,
a lot of money in alimony.
So, he recorded the album
'Here, My Dear' to pay for it.

The artwork on the cover shows a man's hand
passing a record into a woman's hand.
Literally, *'here, my dear.'*
The lyrics offer a personal insight
into the breakdown of the relationship,
sometimes stinging,
at times remorseful.

Some Motown executives
felt it was commercial suicide,
and advised against releasing it.

Gaye ignored their concerns
and pushed ahead.
Sales of the album enabled him
to clear his debt to his ex-wife.

In time, music critics reappraised it
as a flawed masterpiece.

It goes to show
that money is just energy.
You don't own it,
it flows in and out.

You exist with or without it.
It is how you live,
in the choices that you make,
that counts.

So, brands, follow your vision,
follow your North Star,
and as individuals
always try and be yourself.

Follow your heart.
Follow your passion.
And don't always just follow the money.

Chapter 4.

Kind, Clear And Simple

"'Cause love's such an old-fashioned word.
And love dares you to care for
the people on the edge of the night.
And love dares you to change our way of
caring about ourselves.
This is our last dance.
This is our last dance.
This is ourselves."

David Bowie & Queen - "Under Pressure"

The future of business is kind.

If we don't start recognising this
it will be our last chance,
our last dance to fix things.
We don't need more labels
to describe the problems with work.
We need action, now.

There is a countdown clock on my website
of the days, hours and minutes until 2025.

It's a daily reminder
to many a corporation or brand
who proudly promote
their well-intentioned targets,
related to social and environmental policies and goals,

The clock is literally ticking.

It's an opportunity
to be meaningful with some of our 90,000 hours.
To make a difference
to people and the way we work together.

Brands are like little ecosystems.
Everybody has a part to play.
A contribution to make.
Where do you want to do your best work?
In what environment?

There's an opportunity to rethink and rebuild.
Especially if you want to start your own thing.

I believe that kindness
is the #1 regenerative strategy for any business.

Invest in the people that you have.
Avoid the 'burn and churn' mentality.
Be clear in your truth and your values.

If it's not clear and simple,
your people won't understand.
And if they don't understand,
they won't follow.
It's as simple as that.

How complicated you want to make it
is up to you.

Just remember that business is human.
It is about people working for people.

This is our last dance.
We have a chance to do things differently.
Take it. Now.

The Middle

I am striving
to create an impact.
To make work a better place.

To leverage kindness
as the catalyst.
To shine the light
on emerging talent.
The 'Next Generation' of leaders
on the rise.

My observation and experience
from corporate life,
is that a lot of organisations
focus on the top of the tree
with executive leadership,
offering training, support,
paths for career development,
fast track schemes.
Granted,

not everyone has the ambition
or skillset to be a senior leader.

However,
I see the opportunity in working
with the middle management,
those on the rise,
those still finding their voice,
those learning
to navigate their authenticity
in the business world.

Here is where we can create impact.
To inspire a mindset of *kindness*
as an active choice.
To recognize the value
of daily *gratitude,*
and instil the benefits
of maintaining
momentum and *resilience*.

With these *four values* in place,
we can nurture
a positive vibration, globally.

People First

I've always believed
that people work for people.
When they feel secure and appreciated,
they simply perform better.
There is a perception
that fast-paced processes and work cultures,
lead to more risk-taking.
In fact, it's the opposite.

Good leaders need to create a sense of calm and safety.
To give people the courage to take risks.

Your people
are the single most important asset
in any brand, company or agency.

Before your product
or your service,
It's your people.

Without them nothing happens,
you don't have a company
just a name, or an idea.

Companies need to refocus
their commitment to their people.

To show empathy, understanding and kindness.
It's how you inspire people,
build loyalty.
Loyalty and retention increase;
burnout and absenteeism are reduced.

When your people perform better,
your business performs better.

Grow your people.
Grow your brand.

"Corporate is F****d"

This bold observation
was made by a friend (who works as a product designer)
during a conversation they had
with a business contact.

"There's no time for design," they continued.
"Corporate talks a good game,
but when it comes down to it,
there's no time.
It's the same with strategy."

This observation
about the lack of value
placed on creativity in corporate
was further validated
by a client,
who works in the world of advertising.

They were bemoaning
the demise of strategy as a function,
the role and the value

it plays in shaping the work.
To create new ideas.
To shape a different narrative.

To encourage innovation.
To bring fresh thinking.
To make a difference.

Instead,
it was the same old, same old.

This lack of attention
to design and strategy
feels a bit zeitgeisty.

Previously the three tenets
of successful Fortune 500 brands
were rooted in
design,
innovation,
and *demand creation.*

(Think of the likes of Nike, Apple, and Starbucks.)

A lot of business today feels
like there is no time
for creativity,
for design,
no time for strategy,
or meaningful thought
and purpose.

They have been replaced
by other gods;
greed, laziness, and 'speed to market.'

And then there's fear.

Fear of trying something new.
Fear of rocking
the perceived status quo.
Yet it feels at odds
with what people want.

People have changed
(Let's not call them 'consumers,'
they are humans like you and I.)

Their values have evolved,
the things they care about
are different now.

They are looking
for innovation in sustainability,
they are looking
for thoughtful ideas to inspire.

The very output
of strategy, design and creativity
working hand in hand.
There is this disconnect,
this gap between
what people want,
and what the corporate players
and ad agencies are churning out.

There is a culture clash
happening in corporate,
and by default, ad land.

Gen Z's,
along with seasoned professionals
in design and strategy,
are being met
with a toxic façade.

One that claims to care
about the triple bottom line;
people, profit, planet.

Yet they are doing a shocking job
taking care of their #1 assets:
their people.
The employees
who show up
each day for them.
Employees at all levels

are struggling.
The pressure
has never been so bad.

The system so broken.

Designers, strategists and creatives
are burned out,
disillusioned
leaving in their droves.
And they are not alone;
this pattern continues
throughout the organisation.

What is required
is a more human approach
to business,
a more conscious approach,
AKA *conscious capitalism.*
Now is the time
to rethink

organizational design,
ethics,
and values
in the workplace.

To create leaders
that people want to follow.
After all, people work for people.

It's time to slow down.
To listen.
To take risks.
Be bold.
Be free.
Be kind to one another.

Let's change the game together.
'Who's in?'

K.I.S.S. (Keep It Simple, Silly)

Post pandemic,
here's two of the biggest driving forces in business:
simplicity and momentum.

Now is the time,
to cut through the crap.

To practice moving forward,
with simplicity.
There are situations at work,
that become overly complicated
really quickly.
Like a kite string,
all twisted and knotted together.

Imagine if you take the time
to work through the knots,
to unravel the string,
so that the kite becomes untwisted
and can fly again.
Keep it simple.
Keep moving forwards.

Seamless

Kindness is a catalyst.
Use it to find ways to reduce friction.
That way you close the gaps.
And increase potential.

Think Small, Win Big

We have changed.
Work has changed.
Humans have spoken.

The ask is for a more
human approach
to business.
Successful,
future-facing organizations
embrace this mindset.

From an organizational standpoint,
kindness
is the glue to all of this.

It starts with enabling
people to be seen, heard and to be valued,
especially at a time of change
when things are new
or uncertain.

And it starts with being kind to yourself.
Through *Actionable Kindness* ™
this ask becomes clear,
tangible and achievable.

Often the introduction
of a new approach
or strategy
is met with resistance
and obstacles.

Time, resources, and money
spring immediately to mind.

Kindness
is good for business,
good for productivity,
good for revenue.
Ah, maybe that got your attention.
Revenue.

Companies who make the choice
to make kindness
a core part of their culture
and ways of working,
can see and feel the impact.

Kindness
improves trust,
teamwork,
productivity.

It drives
positivity and
performance,
loyalty and retention.

It creates
a future-facing organisation
committed
to inspiring a lasting
impact.

Kindness is the #1 unlock
to grow
both your people
and your brand.

Having a defined purpose
enables people
to feel that their work
has meaning.

When leadership embraces
a mindset of kindness,
it creates a dynamic culture.

One that is propelled forward
with trust and integrity.
To spark change,
you need to have
your people on board.

Maximizing kind,
positive human connections
is key to successful business.

Have a big idea
but start small.
Implement daily actions
that are direct and relatable.

This is *Actionable Kindness* ™
Practice it every day,
because every day counts.

Clarity And Simplicity

At a higher level
it's essential that the purpose
of a brand or company
is simple and clear.

If it's not simple and clear
your employees can't follow you.
And if they're not following you,
then productivity suffers.

People will keep asking
"What's is it that we do?
What is our mission?"

If people don't know that,
then their own contribution
to the company purpose
is unclear too.
So, their experience
is one of uncertainty.

Of not being fulfilled.
Clarity, simplicity and calmness,
are some of the magic ingredients
to ensure well-being
and productivity,
in every brand and company.

And kindness
is the secret sauce,
that binds it all together.

Rethink The Blame Game

Next time you're about to play the 'blame game',
take a look at your hands.
Literally.
When you point at somebody,
you have one finger
pointing towards them,
and three fingers pointing back at you.
In that moment
when you feel triggered to respond,
don't be too hasty.

Pause, take a beat and reflect.
Ask yourself,
"What is my contribution to this situation?"
"Is there something that I could do,
or should do
or didn't do
that contributes to this current situation?"

When the shit hits the fan,
look at your own hands first
before you add to the situation.
That way you can help diffuse more than you can confuse.

Kindness KPI's

My goal is to shift away
from the traditional metrics of success
and achievement in the workplace.

Naturally, revenue and growth are key
to the health and buoyancy
of a company;
after all employees
need compensation and benefits.

However,
my ambition is to establish
true *'Kindness KPI's'*
to gauge well-being,
which has a positive impact
on productivity.

This could be targets
for reducing absenteeism
and burnout rates,

targets
for increasing referral rates
("This is a great place to work"),
for focusing on retention rates,
or for celebrating employee milestones.

These would be elevated
as an organizational priority,
not buried
somewhere in an HR handbook.

Senior leaders
would be actively required
to share KPI's
on how kindness
had a positive impact
on a particular team,
function,
or department's performance
as part of a Quarterly Business Review.

This would be presented alongside
the traditional revenue metrics,
to demonstrate
the health and well-being
of the company,
on an equal par
with its profitability.

A simple step with a big impact.
Actionable Kindness ™ in motion.

Thought For The Day

Chronological age
doesn't define who we are,
inside or outside of work.

Nor should it be used
as a predictor of career success,
ambition,
or drive.

Make It Count

"I don't get it, the job title in the post,
and what they are asking in the job description,
it doesn't add up.
They are completely different.
What does that really mean?
It's so confusing?"

I was recently discussing a post
for a job
that a friend had been sent.
They get approached about a whole range of jobs,
just because they have 'design' or 'creative'
in the title somewhere.

And it got me thinking.
Shouldn't we make things
simpler and clearer,
so that people understand
what they are actually being asked to do at work?
I know, crazy - right?

In the past we had
'The butcher, the baker, the candlestick maker'
to quote the nursery rhyme.

Somehow along the way,
we've made things complicated.
Overly complicated.

Is it in the pursuit of each role sounding grander?
More important sounding?
With this global blah blah role
and that integrated digital thing-a-me-jig.

Or is the perceived importance
of a title
focusing on the wrong thing?

How about we empower people
to understand
that it's what they contribute

to a company that counts?
Not a fancy title, with the new words,
or new descriptions,
that leave people scared to ask,
*"What does that mean?
What is it that you actually do?"*

In a recent survey
85% of employees,
said they were unhappy in their current role.

If it's not clear what they're being asked to do,
is it any wonder they're dissatisfied?

So, today, think about
what you contribute to your company.
It's not about titles.
It should be about being part of something bigger.

It’s not just revenue,
or shareholder value.
It should be about valuing yourself
and your contribution.

It’s about doing something meaningful,
that makes a difference.
To make it count.

The Game Has Changed

There's still too much focus
on perfection in business,
rather than human qualities,
such as kindness,
compassion,
empathy.

We need to challenge
the ingrained facade of leadership
that has been dominant
for many years.
It's no coincidence
that many of the structures of companies,
offices and working hours,
were built on principles of the military.

Post World War II,
when major global economies
needed to rebuild themselves
and their infrastructures rapidly,

they turned to some familiar practices
that had served them well
in times of conflict.
That was nearly two generations ago.

It's understandable that Millennials, Gen Z
and the emerging Gen Alpha,
share an alternate view on things
and relate to the world
in a different way.

Fundamentally,
business is a human thing
and needs to be addressed accordingly.

Kindness
is not a weakness.
It is a strength.

There is no excuse
or exemption
for not being kind.
It's a human quality.

It deserves its place in business.
As it does in every other place in our lives.

How To Move Forwards When There's A Difference Of Opinion

We've all been there.
That meeting or conversation,
that goes round and round in circles.

Everyone passionately
sharing their (different)
points of view,
leading to stalemate
and no progress.

Here's a thought
to sense check
if you're all debating
the same thing:

What is the key question or questions
that you're trying to find the answer to?

By agreeing this upfront,
you ensure that you are all
devoting time and energy,
to solving
the same challenge or opportunity -
even if you don't agree
on the outcome.

Not A Playground

Let's not mince our words.

A 'toxic' environment or a 'toxic' employee
is an unkind environment or an unkind employee.
It is a place of work, not a playground.

All forms of bullying,
gaslighting
and BS 'people' politics
have no place there.

Let's make work
about positive, human connection.
A place to do your best work
ever.

Thought For Today

Unlike Elvis, kindness has not left the building.

Can Kindness 'Cure' You?

Scientific data has shown
that the hormones
related to stress
can impact and down-regulate genes.

The long-term effect of this
is to cause disease.

We know that we can adapt
and develop ways
to control our emotions.
However, as humans,
due to the size of the neocortex,
we can trigger stress responses
by thought alone.

By thinking, focusing and churning
on our problems
we can switch on those chemicals.
Meaning our thoughts alone
can make us sick.

Therefore, if it's possible that our thoughts
can make us sick,
is it possible that our thoughts
can make us feel better?

The answer is '*yes*'.
Acting with kindness
has the potential to make you feel better, healthier.
I'm not talking
happy-clappy unicorns and rainbows here.

I'm talking intentional, choiceful actions.
Developing a positive mindset
to navigate the realities of work.

We call it *Actionable Kindness* ™
Be bold.
Be kind.
Be well.

Join The Dots. Close The Gaps. Grow Your People

Gen Z.
If you want to know
what your next generation
of leadership
looks like,
thinks like and values,
then you better get to know them
quickly.

The future success of your company
is in their hands.

Many companies have up to four generations
working side by side with one another:
Boomer, Gen X, Millennials, and Gen Z.

Practically speaking,
the leadership of those companies
resides with older generations
such as Boomer or Gen X.

However, what this leadership
should be aware of
is that the joint population
of Millennials and Gen Z
is now greater
than all the other generations
combined.

In 2020, Millennials made up
35% of the global workforce,
with Gen Z making up 24%.

That equates to more
than half the entire
workforce population.

Gen Z are the ones to watch,
with more than 2 billion people
in this age range globally.

Having a unifying business strategy
rooted in emotional values
such as kindness,
and where the outcome
is not simply profit,
will resonate with the mindset
of this influential generation.

Take a look at your current middle-management.
Then take a click down
at the people they manage.
It's likely that they will be
a combination of Millennials and Gen Z.

In a recent Microsoft report,
60% of Gen Z's say
that they are merely surviving
or flat-out struggling.

Gen Z also reported
more difficulty feeling engaged
or excited about work,
getting a word in during meetings
or bringing new ideas to the table,
compared to other generations.

The future leadership
of your company
does not feel like it is
being seen, heard, or valued at work.

Read those last two paragraphs again.
To compound the situation,
there is a huge disparity
in perception
of how well things are going
between business leaders
and the rest of the organisation.

In the same report,
61% of leaders
say they are "*thriving*" right now,
which is 23 percentage points higher
than those without decision-making authority.

That's a major discrepancy between
those who are 'saying'
(The leaders)
and those who are 'doing'
(The employees).

This is one example of
'The Kindness Gap" ™
in companies today.

How does your company look like?
The situation of leadership and employees
not being on the same page
might not be new,

but the stakes are significantly
higher today.

The demographic of people at work
is different,
and their values and attitude to work
are different too.
The pandemic changed the face of work
and the role of the office forever,
requiring a new mindset and approach.

It also changed
people's relationships
with work
as a 'thing' in and of itself.

It sparked a global mass exodus
from work
with 'The Great Resignation'
seeing over four million people resigning in April 2021

in the US alone.
So, what can you do?
Find ways to engage
with the younger generations
in your organisation.
Give them meaningful opportunities
and outlets to express themselves.

Importantly, acknowledge
their input,
and provide feedback,
even if you don't know
all the answers.

Start the dialogue.
Take small steps
to bridge '*The Kindness Gap.*' ™

Know Your Role In A Crisis

Everything is great.
Until you hit a bump.

A friend of mine was telling me recently
how their company
was going to miss the quarter.

Sales were down in all areas of the business.
"*Marketing isn't working,*" said Sales.
"*Sales isn't working,*" said Marketing.
Operations looked at some spreadsheets
and downward curves.

Consequently,
everyone started playing
the 'blame game',
and the vibe got ugly,
really quick.

A test of a company's culture
is not when things are going well,
when you're coasting.

It's when there's a kink in the road.
When's there's a bump. A storm brewing.
Or worse.

A ship is designed to sail
in both calm and rough waters.
When things get
a little choppy out there,
you don't see people
pointing the finger,
or jumping overboard.

On a boat
everybody knows their place.
Their role, their function.
Their life might depend on it, after all.

They are battening down the hatches,
they're trimming the sails
leaning into the wind,
riding it out,
knowing importantly
that it will pass.

When we point the finger at work
and play the blame game, ask yourself:

"What am I doing in this crisis?
"What's my accountability?"

We all have a part to play.

Thought For The Weekend

IMPOSSIBLE
I'M POSSIBLE

Small adjustments, big results.
What's a small change you can make this weekend?

The Business Case For Kindness

There's a perception
that somehow kindness
is a weakness in business.
Hold that thought.

Kindness is an enabler
to calm,
supportive working environments.
This inspires trust and loyalty;
it reduces burnout and absenteeism.

Toxic cultures
cost companies billions of dollars
each year.
Let's break down the costs
to replace an employee
who leaves due to burnout.

On average,
it costs a company six to nine months
of an employee's salary to replace them.

For an employee making €60,000 per year,
that's €30,000 - €45,000 in recruiting and training costs,
with roughly €59,000 - €120,000
in overall losses to the company.
That's an average cost of €90,000.

So, if the words, deeds or actions
of one toxic employee,
be it a peer, co-worker or leader,
triggers ten people to leave your company,
that one toxic employee
has cost your company up to €1 million.

Take a moment,
and think about someone you know
who behaves
in a toxic manner at work.

Is that employee
so valuable to your business,

that they *lose* you
that much money every year?
I think not.

Therefore,
is kindness a weakness
or is it actually
the smart choice?

The toxic employee
might be popular
with some people,
or generate sales and revenue.

In the long run, though,
they'll damage your business,
its reputation,
and its productivity.
So do the right thing.
The kind thing.

Let them go.
It'll be a wake-up call for everyone.

Especially them.

It's Everyone's Job

A "*No*" answer
is always better
than no answer.

People work for people.
It doesn't matter which industry, category, or department.
Work is about daily human interaction.

Currently,
I see a lot of debate
between different groups and functions.
HR, recruiters, job seekers, CEOs,
middle managers, juniors,
whomever.

The responsibility
for culture in business
does not reside
with any one team, function or department.

It is up to each and every person
in an organisation
to make a contribution.
To have accountability.
To take responsibility for that culture.

Every day.

Whether we are the one
giving or receiving.

Whether it's an e-mail,
in a meeting,
or via a notification.

We need to act responsibly.
After all, it's how we
would like to be treated.

Not just ignoring people or looking the other way.
Pretending we are 'too busy' to respond.

Behind every piece of communication,
there is a human 'being,'
not just a human 'doing.'

Be kind.
It costs nothing
but it means everything.

Don't Cut Corners

Despite some positive-sounding soundbites,
less than 8% of Fortune 500 brands
have allocated meaningful budgets,
to implement the broad church
of well-being practices in the workplace.

Senior leaders,
if you do not start
addressing these root issues,
you will not have an environment
that empowers your people
to feel good,
and perform at their best.

No amount of ping pong tables,
free app subscriptions,
or healthy snacks in the cafeteria
will fix that.

Start to allocate.
Invest appropriately in kindness now.

Given that 60% of employees
who have been with their company
for eight years or less say they'd change employers
for a more positive, kinder culture,
there's no time to lose
if you want to retain
your best talent.

A Simple Choice

When you have a positive,
kinder, working culture,
people show up to work
with more joy.
Joy fuels productivity.

When your people
perform better,
your business
performs better.

You can measure
the growth in your people,
not just in the profit of your brand.

Isn't this the kind of organisation we want to build:

Teams of well-rounded individuals,
juggling the balance
of their personal

and professional lives,
feeling that their input and contribution
is valued?

Employees who feel motivated,
self-empowered,
enabling them
to move forwards
with speed and kindness?

Is it really such a difficult choice
to make today?

Use Your Own Crayons

A lot of companies
encourage employees
to stay in their lane,
to 'draw within the lines.'

This can be hard
when you are in
this transitional phase of self-discovery
as a leader.

My response is
to encourage them:
Yes, 'draw within the lines,'
but 'use your own crayons.'

To express themselves
in an authentic, open way
that is true to themselves.

For Gen Z, growing up
being radically inclusive,
empathetic,
and openly caring
about the world and social issues,
this notion of being true to themselves
not only
increasingly resonates,
but is expected as the norm.

Leaders
need to acknowledge
this potential generational divide
in approach,
and work harder
not to alienate
generational groups,
but to use the power of kindness
to bridge the thinking,

to establish
more future-facing
brands and companies.

It's how you enable
a culture and legacy
of kindness
throughout an organisation.

Detox At Work Day

Here's a crazy idea.

Imagine if we dedicated one day
where *everybody*
who works in a toxic workplace
agrees to pull a 'sickie',
and not show up.
We call it 'Detox At Work Day.'

Think of the impact
that would have on
productivity;
the sheer optics of it all.

It would highlight
how big a problem
this really is,
on an individual,
national,
or even global level.

It also might scare the crap
out of a few CEOs,
and be enough
to shake them into making changes.

We call it *Actionable Kindness* ™
It's worth a try.
What do you say?

Rethinking SHV

The system is broken.
Time to do things differently.
In business,
'SHV' generally means,
'Share Holder Value'.

It drives many of the decisions
and choices,
not always to the benefit
of the people who work there.

It's often considered
as one of the defining measurements
of success of a company.

Shouldn't we reframe 'SHV'
to stand for
'Seen, Heard, and Valued'?
And create a metric
by which a company's success

is measured not just in revenue,
but in its ability to
See, Hear, and Value
the people who work there?

Now that's something worth working for.

How To Change The Game

Toxic work culture.

Sometimes things are hard to explain, but easy to feel.

Kindness.

Sometimes things are hard to explain, but easy to feel.

Positive work culture.

Sometimes things are hard to explain, but easy to feel.

Change the narrative, change the game.

Kindness costs nothing but means everything.

This Must Be The Place

Why is psychological safety
so important
to the creative and innovation process?

For people to feel comfortable
taking risks,
managers need to create
calm, safe environments,
for them to flourish
and explore
without the threat
of comeback.

Innovation without recrimination.

Don't Over-Think It

Your legacy starts today.
There is no re-run.

Embrace Nature

Life isn't linear.
It's not Instagram either.
It's a cycle, sure.
The sun rising and setting.
The moon rising and setting.

Be more in tune with nature.
Relate to the seasons.
Connect to the four equinoxes
and you'll see life differently.
Some say life is eighty summers long.
Can you remember
what you did last summer?

Can you think
what you are going do
next summer?

Words Without Action Won't Win

I love words.
However,
words without action
won't get you very far
in business.

There's a reason
why I have a countdown clock
on my website.

It's a reminder to companies
who set 2025 targets
to address
urgent social and sustainable goals,
that time is ticking.

Literally.

It's there to encourage us all
to take action every day,

to take a step towards
achieving those targets.

As of May 1st, 2023
there were 611 days
before 2025.

By the time you read this it there will be fewer.

What steps will you take today
towards achieving those goals?

False Idol?

The Great Resignation.
The Great Reshuffle.
Quiet Quitting.
Maybe work was a 'false idol' all along?

Leaders are experiencing
the need to adapt,
if they hope
to attract
and keep the best talent.

Why?
Because at a minimum,
people simply want to be *seen, heard and valued.*
To have their contribution recognized.
Maybe we need to make
the 'idea' of work
a bit better,
if we want people
to work hard at it?

Future Joy

My children are 13 and 15 years old, a girl and boy.
They will be entering
the work force
within the next decade.

My hope and ambition
is that between
now and then,
many of the unhealthy working practices
that contribute
to an imbalance
in personal and professional lives
are weeded out.

That employees at all levels of the business,
from top to bottom
and back again,
have a vested interest,
a personal stake,
in physical well-being and mental health.
And that we don't have to explain

that kindness is a strength,
not a weakness.
That it is actually the smart choice.

My goal is to inspire
future generations
to always come to work
with joy.

Bringing little moments of joy
into every day
can make all the difference
to your people,
and your company.

Let's all start with kindness.
It costs nothing
and makes such a difference.

Especially to me.

Chapter 5.

The (Un)Changing Manifesto

"When the routine bites hard and ambitions are low.
And the resentment rides high, but emotions won't grow.
And we're changing our ways taking different roads
Then love, love will tear us apart again."

Joy Division - 'Love Will Tear Us Apart'

For many people the old saying;
'Love what you do, and you'll never work a day in your life,'
feels unachievable, unattainable.
An easy thing to say, but hard to put into practice.

So historically,
we put our faith in companies
to enable our happiness and fulfillment.

We continue to believe
that there's an equal exchange of time,
effort and emotion,
with companies and organisations.

In reality, many companies
lack the emotional maturity
to be in meaningful relationships
with their employees.

Like a life relationship,
we want our 'partner' (work)
to see us for who we are,
appreciate us for what we do.

And like many a relationship,
the routine bites hard,
the desire fades,
and the ambition becomes low.

Yet still we keep coming back,
wide-eyed,
hopeful that things will be different,
things will change.

Sadly, the pattern remains.
The resentment continues to build
and ride high,
but those emotions won't grow.
During the writing of this book,
there have been many examples
of the company/employee relationship
being tested on a grand scale.

Companies rolling back on their WFH/ hybrid policies;
'Be back in the office or else'
Mass layoffs from Big Tech, the perceived 'winners' during
the pandemic.

And most recently, in March 2023, Silicon Valley Bank
went from being worth
approximately $212 billion
on Thursday,
to being sold for £1
the following Monday.

Further proof if needed,
that the only thing
that you can 'bank' on in life is you.

Life is unpredictable.
Always believe in yourself first.
Always love yourself first.
It's okay to change your ways,
to take a different road.
It's your life; live your 90,000 hours.

The (Un)Changing Manifesto

Anyone who wrote
a business plan in 2007
got it wrong.

In 2015,
if you were asked
in a job interview,
"Where do you see yourself in five years' time?"
you would have answered
incorrectly too.

Few people saw the 2008 financial crash coming,
nor the impact it had
on the global economy.

Similarly,
what happened in Wuhan, China in 2020
was totally unexpected,
despite all the ensuing conspiracy theories
that swirled around.

Things happen
at a scale,
that are beyond
our control.
This is just how it is.

March 2020
was a watershed moment.
Never before had
our health and well-being
been put front and centre
on such a human scale.

As we retreated
into our homes,
our future seemed desperate.
Uncertain.

In that moment
everything changed. Priorities shifted.

Together. Alone.

In particular,
we realised the fragility of work.
The importance of humans
in business;
that people work for *people*.

The role the office once played.

How much time,
energy,
and money
was spent
commuting to and from
that place each day.

In response to the unfolding drama,
we transitioned from
'WTF' to 'WFH'

in a matter of weeks.
Whole industries were impacted overnight.
Travel, hospitality, retail, manufacturing, and more.

We adapted
to new rules and regulations,
for how we shopped
for our food and provisions.

Together. Alone.

We rapidly toggled
through varying degrees
of order and chaos,
trying to make sense
of what was happening.

Governments looked to science for answers.
Tough decisions were taken
to keep populations apart.

Human firewalls
at the expense of the economy.

Collectively putting heads together,
in the race for a vaccination
to slow the spread.
We encountered a 1-2 punch.

The physical toll of the pandemic
and the sad cost to human life globally,
alongside the conversation
about mental health and well-being.

This was the spark,
the catalyst for many.

In 2020,
our relationship with work
changed, forever.

With our very existence under threat,
we naturally questioned
our reasons for being.

For living.

What felt safe, secure.

What brought meaning
to our lives.

Stripped back to the essentials,
our daily lives
were put under the microscope.
What brought us hope, joy, connection?

And in that moment
maybe,
just maybe
we acknowledged
that work

had been a false idol
all along.

Unselfishly we asked,
"What's in it for me?"

For some,
"Do I want to continue living in this way,
let alone just working in this way?"

Punk was a moment
before it was a movement.

The pandemic was a punk moment.
Companies needed to 'adapt or die.'

Social observers scrambled
to join the dots,
to define what was happening
to work
on a grand scale.

In April 2021,
four million people
in the US alone
resigned from their jobs -
in just one month.

This was an exodus
like never before.

It was another twist
in the story
being written
in real time.

People weren't quitting their jobs
necessarily for more money.

No, they were tired
of not being seen,
heard,

and valued
by their current employer.

Enough was enough.

But did *The Great Resignation*
capture the sentiment?
There were well-written articles
about the importance
of purpose and culture.

However,
a large percentage
of companies
were paying lip-service
to the playbook,
rather than a genuine desire
to embrace
a 'people first' culture,
with authenticity and integrity.

It was the equivalent of 'greenwashing,'
but with people.
It coincided with the widespread response
to social injustice,
the (lack of) impact
around environmental issues.

Here,
yet again,
people
were let down.

It was a further example
of diminishing faith
and trust,
in governments,
institutions,
and organisations.

The speed of change,
the desire to be heard,
was too great.

People were crying out
for change,
for a new way of working.

They looked hopefully to companies,
but many were too slow.

They dragged their feet
with the opportunity
to create
'the new normal.'

In part this was due
to a lack of a strong ingrained culture,
that could flex
and bend in the wind.

The shiny company manifesto,
painted on many a reception wall,
just didn't stand up to the scrutiny.

Those companies
with an established sense of purpose,
were able to move
with intent.

Their values resonating
seamlessly
from offline to online
and back again.

So, people took it upon themselves
to make that change.

The reality
that life is short
and precious

was writ large.
Working from home took hold.

We adjusted,
it was hard,
but we did it.

Previously we would
cower from the power,
that companies
held over us.

The archaic rules of productivity,
segmented into
dedicated time slots
across a Monday
to Friday.

New studies
into best working practices
such as four-day weeks,
and reduced commuting times,
highlighted the benefits
to both output and well-being.

Emboldened by this data,
we embraced
a new way of being.

Not just working
but living.
Living our 90,000 hours.

It's unlikely
that we will experience
another pandemic
like this
in our lifetime.

However,
it showed how easily
things could unravel.

It highlighted
how quickly
the human psyche
can shift when it needs to.

From apparent helplessness,
to being resourceful, creative,
resilient.
Simple gestures and actions
resonated throughout
our communities.

With the human spirit tested,
we still came through
the adversity.

It shows what each of us
are capable of,
when pushed to the limits:

That you can bank on *you.*

You did it then.
You can do it again.
You did it then.
You can do it again.
You did it then.
You can do it again.

That you can make
that idea into reality,
to start your own thing

That losing your job
is part of the journey.

That sometimes
things need
to fall apart
to find out
where you are truly meant to be.

That your existence
is not necessarily dependent
on these hours
attached to this thing
called 'work.'

You define you;
your job
doesn't define you.

Nor does your title define you.

We continue
to move forward

step by step.
To focus on the things
that are in our control;

to avoid dwelling
on things
that might well be
out of our control.
The biggest obstacle to progress is ourself.

We were born
to live,
to breathe,
to grow.

That is our innate
reason for being.

It is the gift bestowed
on each of us,

on every human.
Not just to survive,
but to thrive.

To experience
the wholeness of living.
To recognise
that no matter what,
there is always something
that we can do.

It just matters
that we don't give up.
To just keep going.
Knowing deep down
that life may deal the cards,
but it's up to you
how you play them.

Embrace that
life can be a bad hand at times,
but it can be played well.

So,
keep those cards
close to your chest.

Own your shit.
Be present, now.
Win the morning, win the day.

Life is short.
Let's make it a good one.

There's enough time.
Just don't waste it.

Acknowledgements

I would like to thank my sisters Claire and Anne, for their unwavering love and support, particularly in the last few years. *"Bingo - Bongo, we're off to the races."*

Thank you to my 'Personal Board Of Directors.' Those folks that keep me honest, tell it straight, even if it's things I don't want to hear (but are usually right!) - Mark Chalmers, Susie Breuer, Jason Fulton, Ben Sibthorpe, Lucia Hargasova.

Many thanks to Ali Kirby for the design, art direction, and for going above and beyond with research and support.

Special thanks to those who read drafts, bounced ideas and shared insights during the creation of this book – Claire Everson-Davis, Wendy Byrne, Fran Sala, Gregor Frotscher, Carola Frisch, Kerrie Finch, Fiona Cullen, Tom Savigar, Fiona Taylor, Ozlem Tuskan, Claus Raasted, Kim Whyte, Jason Schragger, Priya Priyadarshini

To all my lovely clients – you know who you are. Thank you for putting your faith in me to go on those coaching journeys of discovery with you, much appreciated.

Enjoy your 90,000 hours!

References

75% of Gen-Z's have left a company due to mental health concerns.

Source: National Institute of Mental Health, USA
Published: CNBC.com November 2019

1 in 6 of the working population of The Netherlands are currently out on burnout.

Published: NOS November 2022
Source: TNO: Nederlandse Organisatie voor Toegepast Natuurwetenschappelijk Onderzoek
TNO: Netherlands Organisation for Applied Scientific Research

The impact of mental health and burnout costs the UK economy £35 billion a year.

Source: Centre for Mental Health, UK
Published: September 2017

57% of U.S. and Canadian workers feel stressed on a daily basis, the highest in the world.

Source: Gallup
Published: 'The State of the Global Workplace: 2022 Report.'

The impact of mental health and burnout costs the global economy over a $1 trillion each year.

Source: McKinsey & Company
Published: 'Future of Remote Work,' April 2021

"Being the richest man in the cemetery doesn't matter to me."
- Steve Jobs.

Source: Wall Street Journal
Published: May 1993

'As' - Stevie Wonder.

Recorded: 1974, released on the album "Songs in the Key of Life,' Motown Records, 1976

"Kindness is a language which the deaf can hear and the blind can see."
- Christian Nestell Bovee.

Source: 'Thoughts, Feelings, & Fancies,'
Published: 1857

"You Can't Always Get What You Want" - The Rolling Stones.

Recorded: 1968, released on the album 'Let it Bleed,' London Records, 1969

"If you're going through hell, keep going."

- *Winston Churchill.*

"Nobody ever had a good idea whilst being chased by a tiger."

- *Neil Schambra Stevens, 2020*

"Pretty Vacant" - Sex Pistols.

Recorded: 1977, released on the album 'Never Mind The Bollocks, Here's The Sex Pistols' Virgin, 1977

On average, we breathe 16 times a minute.

Source: John Hopkins Medical

Our brains only have the capabilities to achieve two or three sizable, meaty tasks in one day.

Source: Harvard Business Review
Published: May 2017

In a Financial Times survey only 21% of people said that they felt engaged at work.

Source: Financial Times
Published: June 2022

‘Here, My Dear’ - Marvin Gaye.

Recorded: 1977-78. Released on Tamla Records, 1978.

‘Under Pressure.’ - David Bowie and Queen.

Recorded and released 1981 as a single on EMI Records.

In a recent survey 85% of employees said they were unhappy in their current role.

Source: Gallup, “The World’s Broken Workplace.’ 2017
Published: Staff Squared, December 2019

In 2020, millennials made up 35% of the global workforce with Gen Z making up 24%.

Source: Manpower Group
Published: 2020

Gen Z are the ones to watch with more than 2 billion people in the Gen Z age range globally.

Source: Pew Research Institute
Published: Meghan Grace, “Generation Z: A Century in the Making.”

In a recent Microsoft report, 60% of Gen Z's say they are merely surviving or flat-out struggling.

Source: Microsoft
Published: 'Work Trend Index: Annual Report 2021'

Toxic cultures cost companies billions of dollars each year.

Source: Gallup
Published: March 2019

Gen Z also reported more difficulty feeling engaged or excited about work, getting a word in during meetings and bringing new ideas to the table, compared to other generations.

Source: Microsoft
Published: Work Trend Index: Annual Report 2021

61% of leaders say they are "thriving" right now, which is 23 percentage points higher than those without decision-making authority.

Source: Microsoft
Published: 'Work Trend Index: Annual Report 2021'

'The Great Resignation" with over four million resigning in April 2021 in the US alone.

Source: US Bureau of Labor Statistics

The average cost to replace an employee who leaves through burnout is €90,000 due to loss of productivity, onboarding, training, and team impact.

Source: The Society for Human Resource Management (SHRM)

Despite some positive sounding soundbites less than 8% of Fortune 500 brands have allocated meaningful budgets to implement the broad church, of well-being practices in the workplace.

Source: Fortune
Published: June 2022

Given that 60% of employees, who have been with their company for eight years or less say they'd change employers for a more positive, kinder culture.

Source: Harvard Business Review
Published: 2019

"Love Will Tear Us Apart"- Joy Division.

Recorded and released 1980 as a single on Factory Records.

About The Author

Photo:
Peter Hamelinck

Neil Schambra Stevens is the founder of Mercury Jam Coaching, focusing on well-being and productivity in the workplace.

He believes that people work for people; that good business is achieved by leveraging human values - *kindness, gratitude, momentum* and *resilience.*

He works with creatives, strategists and rising talent in brands and agencies, enabling them to *be seen, heard* and *valued.*

Neil draws on nearly three decades of C-suite brand marketing experience for top Fortune 500 brands such as Polaroid, Vans, Levi's, Heineken, Lenovo and Converse.

He is a regular guest, speaker and writer for podcasts, events and business publications, recently contributing to the #1 Amazon Bestselling book - 'Living Kindly.'

Neil believes in simplicity and the principle of *'Actionable Kindness.'* ™
He lives and runs Mercury Jam Coaching from a houseboat in Amsterdam.

Printed in Great Britain
by Amazon

34044163R00225